Rainbow Children

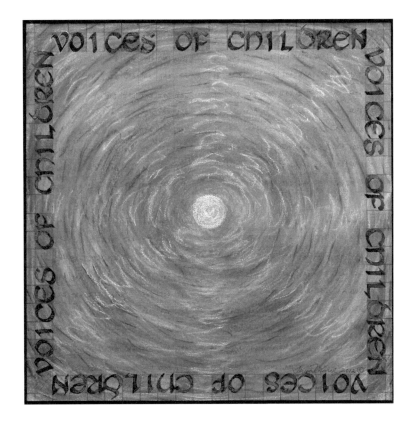

Teresa Marie Staal-Cowley

WestBow Press books may be ordered through booksellers or by contacting:

WestBow Press
A Division of Thomas Nelson & Zondervan
1663 Liberty Drive
Bloomington, IN 47403
www.westbowpress.com
844-714-3454

Interior Image Credit: Teresa Marie Staal-Cowley

Scripture quotations are taken from The Holy Bible, Berean Study Bible, BSB. Copyright ©2016, 2018 by Bible Hub. Used by Permission. All Rights Reserved Worldwide.

ISBN: 979-8-3850-0090-6 (sc)
ISBN: 979-8-3850-0091-3 (e)

Library of Congress Control Number: 2023911216

Print information available on the last page.

WestBow Press rev. date: 07/18/2023

WESTBOW
PRESS®
A DIVISION OF THOMAS NELSON
& ZONDERVAN

Rainbow Children

This story is dedicated to my four adult children and their families. And all the children I cared for in my home, taught art in school, face painted and advocated for in family juvenile court. Rainbow Children is the first of my Voices of Children books series.

The illustrations are painted in watercolors. They have been altered a little to protect the privacy of the children I have face painted on. The children trusted me with their stories, directed me how to paint their faces to bring their thoughts, their concerns, their fears, and their joys out and impart pure wisdom.

12. And God said, "This is the sign of the covenant I am making between Me and you and every living creature with you, a covenant for all generations to come. 13. I have set My rainbow in the clouds, and it will be a sign of the covenant between Me and the earth." Genesis 9:12, 13

Berean Standard Bible

My rainbow is across my forehead and coming out of a dark night with sparkly stars of hope when I used to be very sad and lonely. At the end of my rainbow is a warm chocolate chip cookie with a bite out of it. Miss Teresa, you listened to me last year when you painted my face. You remembered me at the school event with my big brothers, sisters, and mom. Today I brought some friends to get their faces painted.

3

My rainbow is coming out of a dark cloud shedding the tears of my ancestors who suffered on this land. Their tears have covered this land. My rainbow is a sign of hope for my generation, my people, and our native land.

I want to bring peace to both sides, the left and the right, the liberal and the conservative, the whites, and the blacks. I want two rainbows on each side, over my forehead, with me in the middle as a star of hope to bring peace.

I want my rainbow to be a river of clean, flowing water across my face to heal the earth, feed the people, animals, and birds and provide a home for all the freshwater creatures.

9

My rainbow is an ocean wave, because I want to help keep our oceans clean and unpolluted. I want to help make the ocean safe for all the creatures who live there. I want to have fun at the ocean and have it be safe.

11

I want my butterfly painted as a rainbow, because I am working in my family's garden to provide a habitat for the pollinators. We need butterflies and bees to pollinate our food.

13

My rainbow is painted on my left hand to remind me of standing up for peace, and besides I cannot always look at a painted face, but I can look at my hand. Goodbye, see you next time you read another Voices of Children book series.

15

The painting on the cover, Voices of Children, came as an inspiration while doing a work study at Juvenile Rehabilitation Administration (JRA) for Washington State while finishing my senior year at The Evergreen State College (TESC) in 2012. The painting has 400 one-inch squares drawn with colored pencils. In each square, I wrote acronyms inside pertaining to children that I learned at JRA. Over the top I drew and painted the swirls in pastels, watercolor and diluted acrylics. I wrote the lettering with calligraphy ink and a calligraphy pen in an Uncial style. I am a Mixed Media Calligraphy Artist, living in Olympia, Washington with my husband and cat.

Teresa Marie Staal-Cowley

Printed in the United States
by Baker & Taylor Publisher Services